A BEAR APPROACHES FROM THE SKY

a
bear
approaches
from the sky

POEMS

ABBY CHEW

THE WORD WORKS
WASHINGTON, D.C.

The Word Works
P.O. Box 42164
Washington, D.C. 20015
editor@wordworksbooks.org

Cover art: Matt Reynolds
Cover design: Susan Pearce
Author photograph: Matt Reynolds

LCCN: 2018931391
ISBN: 978-1-944585-17-4

ACKNOWLEDGMENTS

Apogee: "Rhona Holds the Girls at Night"
Badlands Literary Journal: "Naming Story," "Cleaving Story,"
        "The Beginning"
Camas: The Nature of the West: "Picket Story," "Road Story"
The Cincinnati Review: "Oolie's Begging Story"
Hawai'i Review: "Dance Story," "Rhona's Sea Story"
Heartwood: "Prologue," "Sister Story," "Oolie's Story"
Hoot: "Coyote's Youngest Story," "Danger Story"
The Maine Review: "Twin Story"
Miracle Monocle: "New Story"
Pine Mountain Sand & Gravel: "Moss Story"
Santa Ana River Review: "Coyote Is Dead Near Exit 202 in Ohio,"
        "Cape Hatteras"
Sou'wester: "Oolie's Visit Further West"
Sweet Tree Review: "Rhona's Nighttime Story"

Thank you to the Ohio Council on the Arts for their support in the writing of this book.

for Ron, the Coyote I met long ago
&
for Alice, the Coyote who was every Coyote ever born

Contents

I have read of two rivers passing through the same lake,
yet all the way preserving their streams visibly distinct.

—Samuel Taylor Coleridge

Prologue

In the beginning, black. It's the old story—ink.
Then a growing out, rip and bloom,
bird unwrapping her wings
one from another There was a world to grow into.

In the beginning came animals not two-by-two,
but one. Discrete. From the one
came caring and anger and water and soil.
From the one came another.
Here he is, a black bear with wings to cover
the sun or the moon or the bed where you sleep.

The Beginning

We are here, in a town
black with leaving—

street covered in fallen shadow, shadow
cut down. A corner turning itself, at this last point, into
something. Kind of crater, place for lost gloves to gather.

Words slide from our mouths like splinters of glass from skin.
"I am full of dying," you say. "I am
the sick black inside a bear's belly."

At the end of this street, particular weapons
are rendered. Crouched down here by the gloves,
spreading my own fingers through the empty fingers,

"Bear's Belly, I would cut the sickness out."

OOLIE STORY

Oolie's shoulders slope, shine black.
Oolie's paws don't move when he walks.
He couldn't retract a claw if he tried.

Oolie's wings.

He grew up in a Pea Island Cove: his mother
taught him about jigsaws and birth, when to sleep and when to leave.

Oolie dances without looking down.
He plays a tater-bug mandolin and taught Coyote
how to cradle the thing in his paws with no scratches to the belly.

Oolie grows hellcat spinach in his garden.

When he was small Oolie chased grackles
down the beach with his mouth wide open.

Oolie learned to fly when the wind flashed in off the shelved sand and
took him up.

Coyote's Youngest Story

Hole in the world where light begins—
crash of thunder and Mother
sliding past with smell and heat—
faster—nothing comes with fall—noses
against my legs with mother's tongue
on my belly—this foot is mine this tail—
in the swirling light
is the hole, blocked back hulk—mother keeps
the light there blood—me with my growl
throat ready in the back—

OOLIE'S BEGGING STORY

Before the world got so damn big,
I held it under my tongue like an aspirin.
Before I got too big, I slept inside a pillbox.
But now we're all bigger. Now I don't sleep much.
I keep an eye on, keep an eye
peeled. Mostly I like things to go just right.
I like to see you hit all green lights
going through town at night.
The hard shot of a home run still rising
as it clears the first deck of seats.
An apple split clean down the middle.
An apple peel all in a coil, one strip
that makes over again the fruit itself, empty.
I like to see the river bend its way to the delta
without leaving its banks to wash away the corn someone
was brave enough to plant in the oxbow
this year. But I like to see the floodplain silted, too. I like the silt
itself. The fine mist of it settling down.
I like it when you bend down to tie your shoe
and find a four leafed clover at your toe.
I laughed out loud when you bowled a perfect game.
I can't get over the way a spicebush caterpillar
tricks me every time—Look! A snake!
I wish our sizes, the world's and mine,
could get it right, too. So I could be in the world,
of it, feeling the silt in the water again,
seeing the ball disappear into the sun
then blinking hard so I could keep my eye
on the place where it would come back into being.

Coyote's Relinquish Story

I am waiting in the highest peak of a golden elm.
This is fall, and I know what it means to wait out the drop.
I have a paw, but I told you it was a hand. I've lied
before. I lied about my age once. I've lied
about car insurance and where I was last night
when I came home and Papa was waiting
on the porch and the ruff around my neck
smelled of whiskey and smoke and something more,
something musky and rotten.
It was the cave I was lying about then,
for the hell of it and for the safety. You guard
a place like that with the bruises on your body.
You do it. I did. You will be glad.

Tangle Story

I read about how photons talk to photons.
How we brush each other, shoulder to shoulder,
fingertips to lips, then move
on, across the whole, the part, the deep.
But the touching never stops; we are never quite
outside each other ever again. We are here.

Einstein scoffed. But I am telling you!
We, the two of us, we are tangled!
We matter. We are matter.
Tiny pull of the moon on my howling in the night,
it pulls her, too. When she struggled
with birth and turned and turned,
I turned on my own axis, but still—I turned!

I am tangled with my own self, too—at once
Coyote and man. I am twisted, raveled, and snarled.
I am never without the hunting teeth.
And thank heavens! Thank the moon!
I am making myself again and again, photons touching photons.

PICKET STORY

The day Coyote's father goes insane,
Coyote climbs a sugar maple in the field
near his cave and watches
for the old man to come. The Father is crazy now
like he's never been before and Coyote waits
in the tree with a rock in his hand.
Sometimes a boy has to kill a man.
Coyote is not a boy and the Father
once made him a fort
with a live-growing blackberry briar fence.

DANGER STORY

Coyote runs through a corn field,
nose up. Right now, with the shout
of blue sky up there and shale
pushing through the furrows,
arrow heads and trilobites,
with the red clay dust,
the heat of every nearby
living thing, he is ready
for the heat to run inside him.

WHAT THEY CALLED THE FEMALE

Rhona born near a barn.
Rhona with a hole in her heart.
One of three sisters.
Rhona red fur.
Rhona like a fox.
Sharp ear. Bloody tongue. Teeth on fire.
Rhona walking fast.
Rhona breathing gasoline.
Who doesn't flinch when the horse fly bites.
One with a male on a leash.
Who tries so hard she pants all night.
One gritty bitch.
Dark as the day is long.
Dreary in the rain.
Jester. Drinker. War Monger. Sniper.
Feather. Chevalier. Perfect little death.

LEARNING STORY

Rhona and Coyote remember every day
flashes of what they saw and how they moved:

Rhona running through a gully on her way somewhere.

Coyote trotting on Shagbark Ridge. Ears high, tail lined out,
lifting his paws like there was nothing so high he couldn't step over.

Rhona sliding herself alongside the underbrush, keeping ready ready ready.

Rhona thinking he'd die that way,
arrogant on a hogback
for all the world to see.

When she disappeared he did not want to hide himself away to find her.

DIALOGUE STORY

I traveled more than a hundred miles from the hill where I was born.

I traveled less.

I could smell you miles and miles and miles away.

You smelled me from maybe a mile away. The wind blew in your favor.

The wind blew in your favor.

The wind favors us.

I didn't know what I would do when I found you.

So we smelled the grass.

We took turns rolling.

We each took a piss.

Yes.

And then we stayed.

Then we hunted mice.

We saw a woman walking on a path with a white dog.

We found a hawk-killed rattlesnake.

We ate some snakes of our own.

We saw in silence.

I still hunt alone some mornings.

You can't give it up.

You don't ask.

Longing Story with Hope

I puff up my feathers and fly in circles.
I stopped eating, flew bigger circles,
started moving on the ground to drag
my claws through the soil, through limestone, sand.
Still nothing. Still no one.
I've hoarded food in fifteen caves in fifteen states.
I've dropped stones from the tops of red oaks,
roared all I have left in my throat, taken on
any threat that may have threatened.
I'm still waiting. Still up here soaring,
casting my eyes ever wider, looking for someone
who can hunt an elk with me, someone
who can take it down with one paw, turn
the belly toward the sky and make an offering,
someone I can offer my own self to.

Dance Story

These were the first pictures ever taken,
blue and grainy, full of the stripes that turn liquid to air.

The girls turned about each other, arms
too short, then too long for their bodies. One twin
with her legs piked up, the other already
turned down, waiting for the way out.

Oolie tells a story
about the older twin, the one that sends
the other one out first—to see, to make sure.

Oolie is half bear, half crow. His arms
shine with feather shoulders camber with muscle.

When Oolie dances late at night,
when Coyote and Mother build a fire and cook a thick stew,
the babies turn over and over
inside Mother, carving their birth names in her belly.

Pocket Story

Coyote had a poker chip, white and worn down around the edges. He kept it in his pocket, its weight against his thigh, pressing through his pants into skin.

Also in his pocket:
1948 Liberty half dollar
any money he might have
three-bladed Barlow pocket knife
2 black and red striped pebbles.

What he kept in a medium-sized hole in the limestone cave:
photograph of Oolie holding the Twins
twisted braid of hair from the ruff of Rhona's neck
2 baby teeth
4 dice, green and white
vole skull.

Coyote lined the hole with tatters from an old pair of coveralls his grandpa wore.

Coyote kept his hands out of his pockets. He never looked in the medium-sized hole at the back of the cave. He didn't want the habit.

BIRTH STORY

The girls: pink-skinned and sharp-eared,
eyes like oil slicks. Their bread-shaped weight
rests on Mother's belly and Coyote's brick-love
heavy in the corner. He lays a paw on Mother's little foot.
He holds a pup up and sniffs her neck, the inside of her ear.
This is how to know them. Mother studies
Coyote's white-lined lips. Tomorrow,
they will stand on the knoll behind the cave,
just east of where the airport used to be.
They'll see quackgrass and wheatgrass and bentgrass.
They'll see trails through the green,
trails made by mice and gophers, maybe even a weasel.
Fox, for sure. Trails that fade before they lead anywhere.
They will see the map of the valley shift.

ACCEPTANCE STORY

Oolie wades into the waves at black dawn.
He measures his steps, lets his wings
shuffle in the water behind. He knew how to catch
salmon from a river before he was born even.
This new thing is a test he's decided on.
He's nearly past the breakers before he starts swimming.
Dive and curl and thrust. He moves
through the swell. He opens his eyes.
He could choose. Could call it out.
Red drum. Bluefish.
Anything. They would come.
Oolie would scoop them toward his jaws,
take the white belly offering.
He does not decide. He lets
water scale through the ruff
around his neck. The sluff of feathers.
Here is the way to swim. And here.
A pelican balances on the edge of breakers.
Oolie flips over to float there where
the dark air and the lit sea meet. He floats.
He lets the swell fill him up.

DEN STORY

Two weeks I spent in the den with them,
just two—little girls with big ears.
Coyote brought us what we needed in a way
I'd never known before. He didn't leave us,
didn't chase the next den, the next heat. He stayed.
And so I stayed longer than I ever had before,
stayed down here in the dark, licking
their sweet faces until their eyes opened,
until I could see who they would be.
Two weeks of turning and turning
circles around them. No dust settled on their toes. I licked it all.
I kept them all to myself. Coyote brought us meat.
It was dark. Sometimes I wanted more air and more light.
Sometimes I wanted to leave. But I stayed. And so did he.

Rhona Holds the Girls at Night

When the wind rattles leaves
down the gulch, she hears planes
flying low. They head further north
to the new airstrip—the one with asphalt,
not this cracked concrete that burrows
deeper and deeper into the honeysuckle,
 Joe Pye weed, and nettles.
There's the particular smell of wet earth,
dry fur, of milk breath.
Rhona walks. Leans into
air the way trout lean into current.
She wants to stay here for a long while,
teaching the twins to stalk
grasshoppers and mice and rabbits.
She wishes she could remember how it was
to hunt that first morning alone,
no sisters biting at her ears.
The grass would've led her on, showed
her how it braided into soil. How
it became tobacco juice
in the grasshopper's mouth.
Rhona sings to her pups now.
She sings a song about how the mouse flipped
from its frantic burrow can land just so,
snicked in a coyote's teeth,
warm and feeding a sharp hunger.

the shrine lies open to the sky

—H.D.

OOLIE SPEAKS

I'm telling you we
are farther back and farther
into everything. We are torchlight,
light flickered, skin
stretched blue at the temple.

Sister Story

When we were very small, we bounded
toward any sound that sounded.
Now we know:
>   quick atop the vole frantic in the sod root
>   away away the rattlesnake shake
>   avoid the tar-smell of the big road
>   follow Mama on the hunt until she sends
>   us out, out to wings to circle on
>   slow and low toward Oolie just landed in the big field.

The other thing we have to know
is how to find each other.

Rhona's Sea Story

shine of fur in black-dawn waves
pelican waiting on a rock with fish tail just peeking from its beak
surfing a wave that turned her upside down but left her on the sand—
nose facing
wide open water
all points to east and all points to west
dance with River Otter in a stand of Yaupon holly
        waxed over leaves and red berries all clustered in her hair
twinge of alone
sheen of glowing across her belly and rocks and her paws and sand
        fighting off the foxfire-memory in the woods by the limestone cave
fighting off Coyote when he came home
and wanted the truth about the other sister
and the night in the woods that made the glow
nestled in her scruff
canoe slice V dash with face in the spray
spine against sand
hands weaving through waves
nose pointed toward Full Buck Moon
        moon shining everything again
                and everyone and no one knowing where the others were
                        but still the water in her hands

SAY

I am not your trickster myth.
I don't have that twist, that trick,
looking for the way
up or out or around.
I want the straight, flinted
heart of the cave.
I want my Rhona and my girls.
I'm looking to know Oolie.
I'm planting, winnowing my way through
the silt on Jack's Defeat Creek,
looking for the black and red painted
stone I know is hidden there. I want that special
place, that special stone, and I'll carry it
in my pocket. I would skin my own self
for a hardened hide armor.
I am my own. I am singing.
This is a kind of shedding, sluffing, molting.
And you have to take me
as this man-Coyote with my life
spinning out here in the field.

Rhona's Relinquish Speech

I can pretend the lines of your face
will fill with water. That a river
will run there, around your eyes
down the length of your nose
spout over your chin.
Fish will come to live
with you, however it is
that new fish come to new water.
You will learn to reach
out your hands to catch
them. You will catch a blue fish.
She will have tiny yellow diamonds
along her caudal fin.
You will be amazed at her curve.
She will turn and curl
and you will love the way.
Later, you will watch
as she turns herself into a blue bird
and then a blue stone.
Don't worry.
You will be standing there
with the river running
inside your skin, stitching
you together. And you have learned
to hold a fish loose and easy
and not worry that she will leap
to dash. You will love her.
She will live for you
in your cupped hand.

JUDGE STORY

Mother Rhona, before she was mother, was Coyote her own self. Running down a lane between two lines of apple trees with one of her older sisters. Rhona stopped to sniff a windfall and stopped again to eat a different, fresher one, and saw the sister lean against a tree with her red hair blowing.

The sister looked at Rhona, and smiled so wide the lines of her mouth made an arc that meant the world was full of the things Coyotes love.

Sister died that fall, gut-shot in a meadow too low on the slope to be safe.

Mother Rhona guards her heart and runs the perimeter of Coyote land with her ears up and her belly near the ground. She's got the air inside her, filtering and screening, holding the best pieces inside for the twins, that they might know where she went and what she gathered.

Welcome Story

No one asks for a cave under an old landing strip. No one asks
for a pack of dogs gone feral from a cluster of farms
three valleys to the east. No one asks for a flood
driving smaller mammals right up to our mouths.
For danger or bounty that leave ruin under their trailing tail.
But here we are, at the mouth of the cave,
fighting off six husky-shepherd mutts, as the whole ark
of mice and rabbits and voles and chipmunks,
skunk and possum, come mewling through the underbrush.

Pulmonary Story

Oolie broke a woman's heart
between his two feathered hands.
He didn't see any other way,
didn't know how to lie anymore.
The woman's heart didn't bleed
as he thought it would. It was a thick but brittle
thing, heavy but easy to hold there,
out away from his body, feel the pressure
building and snap it, snap it with his face
turned away and his eyes tight shut.
He did not tell anyone what he'd done.
He ran a very long way, up the coast very far.
He didn't fly. He kept his legs churning, churning.
When he reached a certain river
he turned left. Oolie's shoulders
heaved but there was no sound in the whole world.
He pulled his own heart out and held it
in his feathered paws.
He looked right at the heavy redness,
snapped it in half, too.
That didn't help a thing.

Cape Hatteras

DH 1979-2002

Coyote wakes me up at 2 a.m.
He taps his paw against my shoulder blade—
he's never looked this old before.
He turns away when I pull on my shorts.
There's the shadow of his back against the wall,
the flash of my white feet.
We start walking
with our faces lifted up.
Coyote says our friend has thrown herself
from her mother's van. She is dying. She will be dead.
I think she must have turned herself
into a kind of bird, a yellow one, extended
tiny linnet wings to swim,
to stretch their sleek pale length toward something dashed
along the swinging curb, the endless curve
of sky that dangled past the swept horizon.
She must have seen her own shape, muscled, flexed,
the body paused in arc as if a hex
were placed there, paused the car's shock and jerk-swerve.
She would have seen the whole world turning just
beneath her elbow. There were her fingernails
mooning white at the ends of her fingers
she hadn't known could be so long. This girl,
dark hair a curtain wind-dashed back
to cover scabbed Cape Hatteras.
Coyote doesn't touch me. He points
to a fist-sized squid rolling in the water.
Out there, just past the charcoaled pier
the sky and water shade into themselves.
No moon. No milk of cloud.
She must have heard her bones hit road, the click
of femur snapped. She would have seen the flare
of pavement, sky, to pavement. Flare of white

that scored itself into her cheek, arm, thigh.
She leapt. She left
us walking Hatteras.
This is how we take the news.
Another few hours, and we'll see the sunrise lighting
up the water and that will be the end.

Road Story

On Oolie's trip to see Coyote,
he sleeps in a culvert with his blocky head
tucked under one wing. He slugs a pint of whiskey,
considers why his feathers just won't sluff the rain.
He walks west mostly, and never toward home.
Oolie can't tell the lines of the sky
from the lines of his own legs.
He sleeps in the culvert, feather fingers tracing circles
on his thighs. There's the smell of diesel,
the rumbling of a semi coming,
and the concrete at his shoulders.

Confession Story

The white of the dog's eye showing as she sleeps.
The blinking of the Summer Triangle
pointed down to me, my face turned up
to meet it. Rhona's nose against my shoulder.
Who am I to own a dog? Who am I to own my own
little self turned helpless and sweet.
I have been ferocious in my need.
I have tamed a pup and kept it for my own.
I have brought this woman home, given her a nest. I've told her we will be safe.
I have made mistakes.
I have killed too often, perhaps,
and with too much joy, for sure.
I've led men onto thin-frozen rivers. It's too easy.
I've chased chickens to see them weeping,
hopping, turning to look,
never facing my bared teeth low to the ground.
It's too easy to be so very bad.
I am beastly. I am too far gone to come back.

Cleaving Story

I walk arm in arm with a demon,
black and feathered. He holds me to the ground,
paw on my shoulder,
keeps my four feet, my two feet, trekking.

I am kissing his hands.
I am licking the paws of a demon.

I am deep in the gullet of the Earth.

I knuckle white stars green stars blue stars
into the darkness we render inside ourselves,
turning this to that, turning tomcats to little pebbles
rolling along an Oregon beach beside a bottle
washed all the way home from Japan. The demon has told me
what it is that circles us all, the stranglehold

of home, of loneliness, of love—I harbor
a love of deep black feathers that rumple up the sheets
we've thrown across our bed. I harbor a hatred of the fear
in the eyes of that woman standing

all alone in the wind-blown grassy field above our cave—that fear
mirrors back again, grows the demon, grows
even the grass in the field until it plaits

back on itself to become the road the demon
crosses with me. I keep my ears pricked.
I'd rather not die—not dash, not flatten, not
become the piecemeal fur and flutter we see along the road.

OOLIE'S STORY

The flying is best at night. The stars
or the absence of stars. The woolen blanket of August heat
or the sheet of sheer February freeze in my lungs.
I say night. But then I think of dawn, the red swell the earth
kicks up on the horizon. I think of early afternoon,
when I can swallow ten thousand gall gnats at a pass.
Early evening, when the chimney swifts column through the mist
settling over Liveszy Lake, rising over the land then falling,
arrowed ground-ward again. There is flight at noon, blinded,
flight just before noon, glazed. It is all my luck to be above it all.

I believe in your power, too, you little ones.
I believe in your hearts, the stretch of your hearts
out toward me, but I do not know how to reach in return
without slicing you bone deep. I do not know how
the two of us can ever meet without breaking.

Hunting Story

We moved in
when the wolves got shot,
their big heads lifted
from the ground between the knees
of proud men with dogs.
We came slowly, moving at night,
following the fresh
scent of newly brave rabbits.
We came when the wolf
hides had been tacked up to cure.
We filled their hole with our own selves.

OOLIE'S VISIT FURTHER WEST

In the cracked bed of Jack's Defeat Creek where you found that
        dogfish skeleton
with its wide-open aching jaws so chockfull of teeth

In the junkyard where you found the hubcap bent in half and
        shining in the light

In the black-dawn when the baby first neck-twists
toward the red waiting light

In the Johnson grass growing in the shadow cast
by the culvert over Scotty's mangled car

Oolie threaded his bird-bear-body through the gap between
        night and morning.

He said the mourner's prayer.
His crow-wings filtered the light—
His bear claws raked rows into the land.

I've seen him in Iowa just
once, when he flew over the river
landed in the band shell
walked out toward the oxbow.
He didn't touch me.
I waited there with my dog. She had her shoulder
pressed against my knee.
Oolie walked with his wings
arced high and his paws up.
He did not touch me. He did not—

Moss Story

I have danced with one foot
on the wall. I have been wrapped
in a wool jacket standing in a kitchen
with my back to the stove and my hand
on a man's chest. I have wrapped that hand
around a burning coal and flung the thing
at my brother's face. In this stand of pines
a small square of skin tangles on a briar.
This is where I'm hiding.
In the steep cliffs and deep hollows.
I will wrap my bones
in birch bark. I will set my skull in the valley
between that oak and my father's barn.
I will cure my hide and make a canoe.
I do not know who will paddle it, but I know
the bow will cut the current like I never could.

FISSION STORY

Oolie knows our separate names.
One of us has a stretch of white along her tail.
One a red tint about the shoulder blades.
We both have black-tipped tails, the yellow eyes that mark us.
One sister, the earth. One, the sky.
He knows who each one is, but he hasn't told us yet.

The grass was belly high and all wet.

—Richard Brautigan

Axis Story

When we were very small, deep in the burrow still,
we lost each other in the dark circle of what was the whole world.
We cried and cried, little howls that echoed back to us,
one after the other, until there was no way to know
if the world was a sphere, with us tilting at the edges,
two poles, across the planet from each other, wishing only to be side-by-side.

Coyote Is Dead Near Exit 202 in Ohio

This morning the hens greeted me at the barn door,
clucking and pecking along, checking my bootlaces
for grain dust, while our four goats
cried from their pen in the corner, climbing the woven wire
gate, little beggars. It's just past Full Peach Moon—
walking home on Christmas night,
I will see a shooting star.
Mars and Orion share a little patch of sky.
I'll reckon you won't believe what I've seen,
though I see it more every day—beauty lies
down in layers. I saw it perched in the Osage orange
over the gob pile on Captina Creek. Coyote is dead.
Every evening I leave the goats
crying in the corner pen, the hens shuffling their knuckled toes
roost-ways into their coop. I'm glad I'm not the morning star,
living thirteen years in eight. I do recollect the snow.
I do stop along the interstate, not to bury Coyote, but to brush
my hand against his little stretched out paw.

What You Didn't Know

Oolie is so beautiful
there is no one who loves him
more than the last.
He is large.
He wraps you in his wing.
He turns over boulders
to feed you grubs for lunch.
You eat willingly.
You do anything.
Oolie. He carries you
if you want. Lets you
pretend you are the one
who can fly and tear
the whole world into pieces.
He flies you so near the sun
you understand, finally, what
light is.
He does not drop
Coyote's pups
when he flies them over the river.
He showed you once,
from way up there,
where the den was.
The black speck of it.
Oolie showed you
a fern that glowed
in the dark woods
they called Spook Light.
He showed you foxfire,
phosphorous, old coal mines.
Down in the gulley
where the cliffs
faded into the river bank,
he laid you down

and showed you
how his wings were
a cape and his claws
could rake just so
up your bare back.

After Sleeping on the Beach

I keep a porcupine quill basket on my shelf.
I've filled it with Oolie's feathers, black and slick.
There is nothing in my pockets but the sand
sticking along the seams. I met him out there
again last night, curled myself into the hollow
between the dunes and waited to hear the swoop
of his landing. The shake and ruffle of his step.
I don't know how to say this.
Oolie and his bird-bear body
blocked out the sky—red dot Mars, seven sisters, Orion.
There was nothing but the black shine.
Standing in that craw, then crawling up the ridge
at dawn, twisting the grass into a braid, learning
new names of water birds and sand grasses.
He had wings and claws and he held me.
I keep a little basket in my house and pray.

Oolie's Mourning Story

I stood behind him when he died,
like I stand right behind all of you, watching.
The sun slashed across the highway,
the snow stood ankle deep—ankle deep for a coyote
trotting down the bank toward his cave.
I was there and I saw him die.
I thought it would happen some other way—
gut-shot in some bramble, pulling his thin body
through the underbrush. I thought he would die
outwitting a man in blue coveralls
carrying a shovel. Trying to live up, show you, show us up.
But it was a semi. It wasn't even beautiful
or just or terrible. Only brutal and fast.
Oh, I did love him. I loved the white fur
lining his ears and lips. His nose
pointed up or down or out, but always
pointed. I did love him. I did. You
were not there. You did not watch his tail
disappear over the bank. You did not
peek over the iron weed to see your little man
running into the black blur of the highway.
You did not see him die. You did not carry
his still slick body across the river in your mouth.
You did not feel his heart beat against your wing.
You did not see the way his ears went limp
the day he saw his daughters born, the way he loved
Mother Rhona, the way he saw the world like it was
burning up and only his looking could save us.
I held him as a pup. I did that. I taught him to howl,
to arch his neck so far the crown of his skull
marked the center of his shoulder blades. I did love him.

Rhona Without

I had a collar once, faded blue with a black buckle.

I wore a collar once.

I wore a collar and I had a little hole in the barn door, a hole with a burlap sack tacked over. I caught mice and chased the cats and ate brown food in a bowl in the corner of the tack room. I did not tell him that. I did not tell him how I knew so much about chicken coops—that the little yellow-haired girl walked me right in the front door to show her Papa I was safe.

I was never safe. I never told him I'd been tamed before. I never told him why my heart was bitter like raw acorns.

Empty Cave Story

On her first morning without him, Rhona
sleeps until dawn, then uncurls her spine
in a slow arc he would have liked. He would have
watched her neck, her legs long, her tail curved.
On her first morning without him, Rhona
cannot see the girls, cannot hear them calling
to each other through the grass taller than their ears.
Their growls become her own moaning.
She catches breaths between great, heaving
vacuums. She imagines him running, lean stretch
low to the ground. She sees him here,
curled in the den, hungry and tired and mean.
The notch in his right ear from a raccoon fight.
The white and black ruff. The perfect mouth.
She imagines him here, sleeping.

Rescue Story

Alone in the cave, I'm tired. He left his dog.
What do I do with a damn dog? She mopes.
She paces our circle home, sniffing,
whining, dancing around, first this way, then that.
She won't eat. She bumps the girls out of her way.
The girls, who still hunger. Who still cry and fight.
They tussle. Even though we are alone, they tussle.
The dog won't eat. Tell me what to do.

Badger Story

We're fast, it's true. The ol' stop and dodge.
But digging, we never got it down.
Oolie brought our new minus-one
family to a badger burrow on a plain we'd never seen.
Badger, mean as a snake, came sniffing slowly
through the flax and rye to show us
just what a badger can do. So now
we hunt together, the chasers and the digger,
sometimes five rabbits in a day,
three prairie dogs, anything that runs aground
to hide—we've got it out and eaten, the team of us.

Rhona's Nighttime Story

I dreamed I was a milking maid.
I loved the animals, loved their wet, heavy noses.
I dreamed I had a milking stool, two arms five legs.
Strange to be spine upright but good too,
to see the world this way.

AT THE FIRE MILL

At the fire mill no one curries favor.
We all lie down to burn
but burning never works.
We walk for miles with our shoes
blazing, touching our toes
to dry brome, going up
like little pails of kerosene,
we kick and spark and snap,
pat the little flames, walk on.
Everyone's learning to build a fire,
smoky at first, but soon enough
raging the whole world over.

Obsession Story

In the dark of the basement, I saw
the sunset through the east window.
It bounced onto the side of the garage
and back again, to me, so that I see
the tunnels dug all around my feet.

KITCHEN STORY REVISITED

Downstairs, I can hear Oolie bearing his bulk
through the cupboards. It's November. He's hungry.
I baked a pumpkin pie last night—I used twice the eggs
the recipe called for. That's how Gramma
did it and that still seems the best way—everything
firmed up in the middle. If Oolie gets his paws
on that pie he'll eat the whole damn thing.
That won't be the end, but it will be close.
We'll go at each other's bellies and throats.
I will bake another pie and take
it to my mother's for dinner.
I will show her the marks
on my shoulder where Oolie grabbed ahold.
"Look at that," I'll say. "Just look at that."

New Story

I saw you in the city last night.
You stalked a rat who bustled
his way through a garbage bag,
eating doughnut halves.
I stalked you.
I watched from the fire escape
while you crept.
Your ears up. Your tail out straight.
Your body stretched
along the line
begun by the point
of your nose
low to the pavement.
When you pounced,
my heart seized.
You were up and back
already, the rat's tail
whipping your eyes. And then
nothing moved
but the muscles of your throat.

Love Story

The light slanting across the church steeple.
The lake slashing light back again,
stockyard and cobbler and grain elevator.
In the distance
—a city—scratching and piercing the blue.
Well, of course smog
or something else gray and hanging low.
There is dark. There is silt.
We are each of us
smudges edged against bright sky.

February Story

Rhona licks the place where a thorn
slid under the pad of her right paw.
She licks and licks and cannot stop
for the pain that comes up stabbing.
Press harder. Chew. Take a little piece of skin away
with the thing itself.

Rhona wishes she knew who
was coming next who might be the one
to meet up with her on the trail
beside the old school house and take to catching
mice or dancing or going for long drives in August
when the milkweeds spit floss across the road.

Later, when she listens to mice mischiefing
under the snow, when she turns her head
just so, when she marks where
and how to kill one little mouse there beneath her,
she will forget about meeting another on a trail somewhere.
She will, instead, enter into the taste and cold and heat
and who she is right then, good, alone.

TWIN STORY

We grew up first in the dark.
We grew up then in the thick overhang
of trumpetcreeper. We grew
thick ruffs around our necks
to protect us from the throat-
slash of other teeth. We grew
faster than spring. We grew faster
than even you, watching us, could see.
We are here now. Our legs ten feet tall.

Naming Story

Oh, you know the collective thing is called murder.
Here we sit, all in a row on a line strung along the road,
ominous, marking your just ahead demise.
But we are also horde. We are also storytelling.
The other half—a sloth. A parcel. A sleuth.
And it's true—I surely ain't a shrewdness.
I swooped low over a tower of giraffes, but I myself
am not a tower. Not a richness of martens.
I've never sought a mate in a harem of seals.
I have flown into a wedge of swans, but only
to snap their already trembling V.
A prickle of hedgehogs? Please.
A wisp, a host, an intrusion.
Shiver. Hover. Watch.
A kettle, a nest, a plague.
I'm every single one.
Who ever saw a group of bears moving
slowly together, just gallumping along?
Anyone? Enough to name us so?
And what if you saw a group of me?
All shuffle-winged and claw-pawed?
What if you saw us moving across the plain,
a row of us—one behind the other? Shoulder to shoulder?
What if you saw us cresting a rise? What then?
But there is only one. There is only me.
And I have a name already.

Departure Story

On the hilltop above the den, we mount
a tor and stop to pant.
We tell each other what the bell ringing
from the church tower means.
We don't know. We tell the stories anyway.
A bell marks time. Or death.
Or the birth of a queen. Look at our raggedy coats!
Flea-bitten queens for sure.
We've grown out of our dugout shelter,
out of the hanging valley,
onto this stone shelf that tips the wind
straight into our ears. From here,
land falls out and away, first deep heart green
then the gray trimline the flood
left as it crept back down the hill. Behind us
the hills keep rolling. We don't know
where they stop. Maybe the same place
the bell stops being heard.
We figure one will head down and one will go back,
to find out, each on her own,
what happens past the bell's trimline,
where new myths bubble up like magma-heated water,
steaming and smelling of minerals,
voices dissolved and transformed into lessons,
warnings, moments of charged life
that will not die alone without being told.

About the Author

Abby Chew is the 2013 winner of the Orlando Prize for poetry and the author of one previous collection, *Discontinued Township Roads*. Her poems have appeared in journals including the *Camas: The Nature of the West*, *Cincinnati Review*, *Heartwood*, *Sou'wester*, and *Sweet Tree Review*. An Indiana native, she teaches English at Crossroads School in Santa Monica, California.

About the Artist

Matt Reynolds studied filmmaking at the University of Miami. Today he edits television shows in Los Angeles and continues to draw, working mostly in pencil and pen and ink. In 2015, he married a poet.

About The Word Works

The Word Works, a nonprofit literary organization, publishes contemporary poetry and presents public programs. Other imprints include the Washington Prize, International Editions, and the Hilary Tham Capital Collection. A reading period is also held in May.

Monthly, The Word Works offers free literary programs in the Chevy Chase, MD, Café Muse series, and each summer, it holds free poetry programs in Washington, D.C.'s Rock Creek Park. Annually in June, two high school students debut in the Joaquin Miller Poetry Series as winners of the Jacklyn Potter Young Poets Competition. Since 1974, Word Works programs have included: "In the Shadow of the Capitol," a symposium and archival project on the African American intellectual community in segregated Washington, D.C.; the Gunston Arts Center Poetry Series; the Poet Editor panel discussions at The Writer's Center; and Master Class workshops.

As a 501(c)3 organization, The Word Works has received awards from the National Endowment for the Arts, the National Endowment for the Humanities, the D.C. Commission on the Arts & Humanities, the Witter Bynner Foundation, Poets & Writers, The Writer's Center, Bell Atlantic, the David G. Taft Foundation, and others, including many generous private patrons.

The Word Works has established an archive of artistic and administrative materials in the Washington Writing Archive housed in the George Washington University Gelman Library. It is a member of the Council of Literary Magazines and Presses and its books are distributed by Small Press Distribution.

wordworksbooks.org

OTHER WORD WORKS BOOKS

Annik Adey-Babinski, *Okay Cool No Smoking Love Pony*
Karren L. Alenier, *Wandering on the Outside*
Karren L. Alenier, ed., *Whose Woods These Are*
Karren L. Alenier & Miles David Moore, eds.,
      Winners: A Retrospective of the Washington Prize
Christopher Bursk, ed., *Cool Fire*
Willa Carroll, *Nerve Chorus*
Grace Cavalieri, *Creature Comforts*
Barbara Goldberg, *Berta Broadfoot and Pepin the Short*
Akua Lezli Hope, *Them Gone*
Frannie Lindsay, *If Mercy*
Elaine Magarrell, *The Madness of Chefs*
Marilyn McCabe, *Glass Factory*
JoAnne McFarland, *Identifying the Body*
Kevin McLellan, *Ornitheology*
Leslie McGrath, *Feminists Are Passing from Our Lives*
Ann Pelletier, *Letter That Never*
Ayaz Pirani, *Happy You Are Here*
W.T. Pfefferle, *My Coolest Shirt*
Jacklyn Potter, Dwaine Rieves, Gary Stein, eds.,
      Cabin Fever: Poets at Joaquin Miller's Cabin
Robert Sargent, *Aspects of a Southern Story*
      & A Woman from Memphis
Miles Waggener, *Superstition Freeway*
Fritz Ward, *Tsunami Diorama*
Amber West, *Hen & God*
Nancy White, ed., *Word for Word*

Nathalie Anderson, *Stain*

Mel Belin, *Flesh That Was Chrysalis*

Carrie Bennett, *The Land Is a Painted Thing*

Doris Brody, *Judging the Distance*

Sarah Browning, *Whiskey in the Garden of Eden*

Grace Cavalieri, *Pinecrest Rest Haven*

Cheryl Clarke, *By My Precise Haircut*

Christopher Conlon, *Gilbert and Garbo in Love*
     & *Mary Falls: Requiem for Mrs. Surratt*

Donna Denizé, *Broken like Job*

W. Perry Epes, *Nothing Happened*

David Eye, *Seed*

Bernadette Geyer, *The Scabbard of Her Throat*

Barbara G S. Hagerty, *Twinzilla*

James Hopkins, *Eight Pale Women*

Donald Illich, *Chance Bodies*

Brandon Johnson, *Love's Skin*

Thomas March, *Aftermath*

Marilyn McCabe, *Perpetual Motion*

Judith McCombs, *The Habit of Fire*

James McEwen, *Snake Country*

Miles David Moore, *The Bears of Paris*
     & *Rollercoaster*

Kathi Morrison-Taylor, *By the Nest*

Tera Vale Ragan, *Reading the Ground*

Michael Shaffner, *The Good Opinion of Squirrels*

Maria Terrone, *The Bodies We Were Loaned*

Hilary Tham, *Bad Names for Women*
     & *Counting*

Barbara Ungar, *Charlotte Brontë, You Ruined My Life*
     & *Immortal Medusa*

Jonathan Vale, *Blue Cowboy*

Rosemary Winslow, *Green Bodies*

Michele Wolf, *Immersion*

Joe Zealberg, *Covalence*

Nathalie F. Anderson, *Following Fred Astaire*, 1998

Michael Atkinson, *One Hundred Children Waiting for a Train*, 2001

Molly Bashaw, *The Whole Field Still Moving Inside It*, 2013

Carrie Bennett, *biography of water*, 2004

Peter Blair, *Last Heat*, 1999

John Bradley, *Love-in-Idleness: The Poetry of Roberto Zingarello*, 1995, 2ND edition 2014

Christopher Bursk, *The Way Water Rubs Stone*, 1988

Richard Carr, *Ace*, 2008

Jamison Crabtree, *Rel[AM]ent*, 2014

Jessica Cuello, *Hunt*, 2016

Barbara Duffey, *Simple Machines*, 2015

B. K. Fischer, *St. Rage's Vault*, 2012

Linda Lee Harper, *Toward Desire*, 1995

Ann Rae Jonas, *A Diamond Is Hard But Not Tough*, 1997

Susan Lewis, *Zoom*, 2017

Frannie Lindsay, *Mayweed*, 2009

Richard Lyons, *Fleur Carnivore*, 2005

Elaine Magarrell, *Blameless Lives*, 1991

Fred Marchant, *Tipping Point*, 1993, 2ND edition 2013

Ron Mohring, *Survivable World*, 2003

Barbara Moore, *Farewell to the Body*, 1990

Brad Richard, *Motion Studies*, 2010

Jay Rogoff, *The Cutoff*, 1994

Prartho Sereno, *Call from Paris*, 2007, 2ND edition 2013

Enid Shomer, *Stalking the Florida Panther*, 1987

John Surowiecki, *The Hat City After Men Stopped Wearing Hats*, 2006

Miles Waggener, *Phoenix Suites*, 2002

Charlotte Warren, *Gandhi's Lap*, 2000

Mike White, *How to Make a Bird with Two Hands*, 2011

Nancy White, *Sun, Moon, Salt*, 1992, 2ND edition 2010

George Young, *Spinoza's Mouse*, 1996

THE TENTH GATE PRIZE

Jennifer Barber, *Works on Paper*, 2015
Lisa Lewis, *Taxonomy of the Missing*, 2017
Roger Sedarat, *Haji As Puppet*, 2016
Lisa Sewell, *Impossible Object*, 2014

INTERNATIONAL EDITIONS

Kajal Ahmad (Alana Marie Levinson-LaBrosse, Mewan Nahro
     Said Sofi and Darya Abdul-Karim Ali Najin, trans.,
     with Barbara Goldberg), *Handful of Salt*
Keyne Cheshire (trans.), *Murder at Jagged Rock: A Tragedy by*
     Sophocles
Jeannette L. Clariond (Curtis Bauer, trans.), *Image of Absence*
Jean Cocteau (Mary-Sherman Willis, trans.), *Grace Notes*
Yoko Danno & James C. Hopkins, *The Blue Door*
Moshe Dor, Barbara Goldberg, Giora Leshem, eds.,
     The Stones Remember: Native Israeli Poets
Moshe Dor (Barbara Goldberg, trans.), *Scorched by the Sun*
Lee Sang (Myong-Hee Kim, trans.), *Crow's Eye View:*
     The Infamy of Lee Sang, Korean Poet
Vladimir Levchev (Henry Taylor, trans.), *Black Book of*
     the Endangered Species

www.ingramcontent.com/pod-product-compliance
Lightning Source LLC
Chambersburg PA
CBHW030854090426
42737CB00009B/1229